FOOTBALL'S
Wackiest
Moments

DAVID
FOGEL

DAVID
Page L

FOOTBALL'S
Wackiest
Moments

Michael Pellowski
Illustrated by Sanford Hoffman

Sterling Publishing Co., Inc.
New York

Library of Congress Cataloging-in-Publication Data

Pellowski, Michael.

    Football's wackiest moments/Michael J. Pellowski: illustrated by Sanford Hoffman

    p.   cm.

    Includes index.

    Summary: Describes amusing anecdotes and crazy quotes involving some well-known NFL coaches, quarterbacks, defensive players, and runners and receivers.

    ISBN 0-8069,1363-0

    1. Football–United States–Acecdotes–Juvenile literature.

    2. Football–United-States--Humor–Juvenile literature.

    {1.Football–Miscellanea.} I.Hoffman, Sanford, ill. II. Title.

    GV950.5.P45 1998

    796.332'0973-dc21

                                                   98-26001

                                                         CIP

                                                           AC

10 9 8 7 6 5 4 3 2 1

Published by Sterling Publishing Company, Inc.

387 Park Avenue South, New York, N.Y. 10016

(c) 1998 by Michael Pellowski

Distributed in Canada by Sterling Publishing

c/o Canadian Manda Group, One Atlantic Avenue, Suite 105

Toronto, Ontario, Canada M6K 3E7

Distributed in Great Britain and Europe by Chris Lloyd

463 Ashley Road, Parkstone, Poole, Dorset, BH14 0AX, United
    Kingdom

Distributed in Australia by Capricorn Link (Australia) Pty Ltd.

P.O. Box 6651, Baulkham Hills, Business Centre, NSW 2153, Australia

Manufactured in the United States of America

Sterling ISBN 0-8069-1363-0

CONTENTS

DEDICATION

To my uncle Charles "Muscles" Pellowski, who served in the Silent Service during World War II, and "Big" John Pellowski, who also served during World War II

INTRODUCTION

American football, one of the world's toughest games, is also one of the world's wackiest sports. During the 125 plus years it has been in existence, this sport has produced a plethora of kooky coaches, loony linemen, wacky runners and receivers, daffy defenders, and enough goofy gridiron incidents to fracture the funny bones of football's most stoic followers. So, sport fans, strap on your chin straps and prepare to be knocked silly by some of pro football's funniest stories. You're all invited to participate in the Super Bowl of Gridiron Snickers.

Michael J. Pellowski

THOSE KOOKY QUARTERBACKS

UNDEFEATED

Pro football quarterbacks are a special breed of athlete. It isn't easy for a pro quarterback to admit defeat. NFL Hall of Fame quarterback Bobby Layne, who played for the Detroit Lions in the 1950s, best demonstrated the winning attitude of a professional signal caller when he said, "I never lost a ball game, but sometimes time has run out on me."

ROGER, THE LEDGE DODGER

Roger Staubach of the Dallas Cowboys had a reputation as an All-American boy during his signal-calling days in the NFL. However, Roger did slip occasionally. Once he had an appointment with Cowboys owner Tex Schramm. When Roger arrived, he was kept waiting in an outer office while Tex completed a long-distance phone call. Roger waited and waited and waited for Schramm to complete the call. Finally, an impatient Roger Staubach decided to let the team owner know he'd arrived. He crawled out an open window onto a three-foot-wide ledge eleven stories above the ground. Roger inched his way down the ledge until he was in front of the window that faced Tex Schramm's desk. It's hard to imagine Schramm's shock when he spied his star quarterback perched precariously outside on the ledge. Needless to say, Staubach wasn't kept waiting any longer.

FUNNY CALL

In 1989, Tampa Bay Buccaneers backup quarterback Joe

Ferguson was named one of America's sexiest men by a female newspaper columnist. When Ferguson was asked what his wife thought about the honor, Joe replied, "My wife hasn't said too much about it—since she stopped rolling on the floor laughing."

SPECIAL GUY

NFL Hall of Fame quarterback Johnny Unitas, who played for the Baltimore Colts, once quipped, "Specialists never practice their specialty too much."

BRAIN WAVE

The Detroit Lions met the Green Bay Packers for their traditional Thanksgiving gridiron clash in 1962. The Packers came into the contest unbeaten in 19 consecutive games and were huge favorites. Unfortunately for the Packers, the Lions staged an astonishing upset in the Turkey Day contest. One reason for the unexpected Detroit victory was that the Lions' defensive line harassed and hammered Green Bay quarterback Bart Starr from the start of the game until the finish. The fable Packer offense was inept for most of the contest

Finally, a frustrated Bart Starr vented his frustration on the referee. "Hey, ref," Starr shouted. "If you give us any more lousy calls, I'm going to bite that big, fat head of yours off."

The referee looked over at the Packer quarterback and calmly replied, "Starr, if you do you'll be the only quarterback in the league with more brains in his stomach than his head."

After that witty remark, Bart Starr kept his complaints about calls to himself.

PRAISEWORTHY

Sportscaster Phyllis George thought Cleveland Browns quarterback Brian Sipe was quite a player in the 1980s. "Brian Sipe is a great quarterback," said Phyllis. "I don't think he's overrated enough."

HEY, COMRADE!

When the Chicago Bears played the Cincinnati Bengals in 1989, Bears quarterback Mike Tomczak came face to face with the Bengals' strong safety, David Fulcher. Tomczak and Fulcher exchanged heated words. When asked about the conflict after Chicago beat Cincinnati 17–14, Mike Tomczak had this explanation: "He said something about how he was coming after me, about how he was going to knock me out of the game—you know, the usual NFL type of camaraderie."

GO FOR IT!

Running back Roger Craig of the San Francisco 49ers was teamed with scrambling quarterback Randall Cunningham of the Philadelphia Eagles in the 1989 Pro Bowl. Craig explained Cunningham's unique style of play this way: "I didn't know whether to block or to go out to receive, so finally I just shouted, 'Go, Randall, Go!'"

CALL THE PLAY

A reporter once asked quarterback Norm Van Brocklin of the Los Angeles Rams what his favorite play was. "*Our Town*, by Thornton Wilder," Van Brocklin answered.

RAW DEAL

Eddie LeBaron only stood five feet, seven inches tall, but that

11

didn't stop him from playing quarterback for the NFL's Dallas Cowboys in the 1960s. LeBaron stood tall on the field and had a tough-guy attitude. Once, Eddie was seated between two huge offensive linemen at a team meal.

"I want my steak rare, red rare," one lineman told the waiter.

"I want my steak dripping blood," the other hulk told the waiter.

"And how would you like your steak, sir?" the waiter asked Eddie LeBaron.

"Don't bother to cook mine," instructed the Dallas signal caller. "Just turn a bull loose and I'll rip off a hunk as he goes by."

BENCH STAR

Reserve quarterback Cliff Stoudt of the Pittsburgh Steelers received two Super Bowl rings despite the fact that he didn't play in a single regular or post-season NFL game from 1977 to 1980. Stoudt sat on the bench for three years as reserve backup to Hall of Fame quarterback Terry Bradshaw. Cliff finally got a taste of NFL action on October 5, 1980, when the Steelers bested the Chicago Bears and Stoudt briefly replaced starter Terry Bradshaw.

QUARTERBACK POTENTIAL?

Bill Kenney of the Kansas City Chiefs appeared in the 1983 Pro Bowl as a quarterback. However, the six-foot, four-inch, 220-pound gridiron star once had difficulty convincing NFL scouts which position he should play in the pros. After his college career ended, pro scouts wanted Kenney to switch from quarterback to tight end because of his size. Kenney had argument after argument with scouts about his future position. One scout from the Atlanta Falcons even gave Bill a written test to determine his gridiron appitude.

"How did I do?" Bill Kenney asked after the test.

The Falcons' scout looked at Kenney and replied, "Very well...for a tight end!"

Nevertheless, despite all the doubts of the so-called experts, Bill Kenney became a Pro Bowl NFL quarterback.

RETIRED PLAYER

In 1993, free-agent quarterback Jeff Hostetler of the New York Giants left the East Coast to play for the Los Angeles Raiders. As soon as Hostetler arrived in Los Angeles, he proved to be a big help to the Raiders' club. While Jeff was driving to camp from the airport with Raiders quarterback coach Mike White and team Director of Operations Steve Ortmayer, the car the trio was in got a flat tire. Neither White nor Ortmayer could fix the flat. It was new quarterback Jeff Hostetler who changed the tire.

13

QUARTERBACK ROTATION

Charles Conerly and Don Heinrich were quarterbacks on the 1956 New York Giants football squad. Conerly was the better athlete and had a strong arm, but Heinrich was a shrewd student of the game, able to read and pick apart opposing defenses extremely well. To best utilize the talents of both signal callers, the Giants' staff came up with a wacky plan that worked. Don Heinrich started the games that season and remained in until he figured out the opponent's defensive scheme. Don would then remove himself from the game and tell Charlie Conerly which plays would work. Conerly was then inserted into the game while Heinrich sat on the sidelines. The two-quarterback rotation helped lead the Giants to the NFL Championship.

APPROPRIATE NAME

In 1953, the Chicago Bears had a quarterback on their roster named Willie Thrower.

TALK LOUDER

In September of 1980, San Francisco 49ers quarterback Steve DeBerg contracted laryngitis. After screaming out signals in a victory over the New Orleans Saints, DeBerg almost totally lost his voice. During the week of practice before the 49ers' next game, against the St. Louis Cardinals, DeBerg's teammates couldn't hear his cadence calls at the line. Since DeBerg was too valuable to the team to be replaced, the San Francisco squad got permission from the NFL to solve their sound problem. Steve DeBerg's helmet was wired with a special microphone that amplified his voice loud enough for his teammates to hear his calls. With the help of his microphone helmet, soft-spoken Steve DeBerg led the 49ers to a 24 to 21 win over the Cardinals.

RUN FOR IT!

Pittsburgh Steelers quarterback Terry Bradshaw once made this comment about his style of broken-field running. "I'm a cross between a fullback and a sissy," said Bradshaw.

HOW YA DOIN'?

Craig Morton was quarterback for the Denver Broncos in a game against the New York Giants in 1980 when the ball slipped out of the Denver center's hand during a snap. Instead of a pigskin, the hand of the Broncos' center ended up in the grasp of quarterback Morton.

"What could I do?" Morton said to reporters after the game. "I shook his hand and said, 'How you doing?'"

COINING A PHRASE

In 1989, the Dallas Cowboys had three quarterbacks on their roster. The signal callers were veteran stars Troy Aikman and Steve Walsh, along with backup Babe Laufenberg. At the beginning of the season both Aikman *and* Walsh were listed as the team's No. 1 quarterback. One day, Babe Laufenberg explained to the press how Dallas might have to eventually decide just who the squad's starting field general would be.

"I really think it's going to be a coin flip," stated Babe. "And I get the call if the coin lands on its edge."

OUCH!

Pittsburgh Steelers reserve quarterback Cliff Stoudt did not play in a single NFL football game from 1977 to 1980. Nevertheless, Cliff tore a ligament in his ankle during that period. Stoudt suffered the injury playing for the Steelers' off-season basketball team.

ON YOUR GUARD

When John Elway, the great Denver Broncos quarterback, was just a rookie, he made one of the most embarrassing goofs a pro signal caller can commit. It happened in 1983 in a lop-sided gridiron contest against the San Diego Chargers. The Chargers were leading by a large margin, and Elway was being hammered and harassed throughout the contest by the Chargers' defense. In the fourth quarter of the blowout, Elway broke the huddle. He looked over the defense and then made his big mistake. John walked up behind his left guard Tom Glassic and reached down to take the snap. Of course, a sur-prised Glassic didn't have the ball; center Bill Bryan did.

"Over here!" Bryan yelled to Elway. A rattled and embar-rassed John Elway quickly switched spots, took the snap from Bill Bryan, and promptly fired an incomplete pass out of bounds.

CATCH UP

In 1959, quarterback Milt Plum of the Cleveland Browns completed a 20-yard pass in a game against the Chicago Cardinals. What makes the play unusual is that Plum completed the pass to himself. During the gridiron contest, Milt Plum dropped back to pass. A Chicago defender blocked the pass, knocking it back toward Milt. Plum plucked the ball out of the air and raced downfield for a 20-yard gain.

YES, COACH!

Coach George Halas of the Chicago Bears was the kind of guy who demanded and got strict obedience from all his players, including his quarterbacks. When quarterback Bernie Masterson first joined Chicago, Halas gave him some strict instructions before putting him into a game. "Run the first play over right tackle," Coach Halas ordered. "Run the next play around left end. And then after that, punt," Halas said.

Masterson ran into the game. Following orders, he broke the Bears' huddle deep in his own territory and then ran a play over right tackle. The Bears' runner broke through the line and scampered to midfield for a first down. On the next play, Masterson again followed Halas' instructions and went around left end. The run resulted in a first down at the opponent's 15-yard line. With the goal line in sight, quarterback Bernie Masterson then called for a punt, which sent the football into the stands behind the end zone. This is a case in which one of his players followed Halas' instructions too closely.

STRANGE PREMONITION

For a long time, Jim McMahon was the star quarterback of the Chicago Bears. In August of 1987, McMahon posed for a publicity poster dressed as General MacArthur. He was standing near a duffle bag and holding a football. The caption below him read, "I shall return!" This meant that McMahon would take the Bears once again to the Super Bowl that season, which was to take place in the city of San Diego. However, Jim McMahon was later traded to the San Diego Chargers. Oddly enough, printed on the duffle bag seen in the Bears' 1987 publicity poster of McMahon were the words "Destination: San Diego"! Perhaps these words were a forecast of McMahon's future gridiron home.

SPEEDY CALL

In 1996, Indianapolis Colts quarterback Jim Harbaugh earned in the neighborhood of four million dollars for playing pro football. That same year, an Indiana State trooper stopped Harbaugh for exceeding the speed limit and gave him a ticket. As the trooper handed Harbaugh the summons he quipped, "It's a 25-dollar fine. I think you can afford it."

WHOOPS!

In 1994, *New Jersey Monthly* magazine featured New York Giants quarterback Phil Simms on its July cover and called Phil "the last of the true-blue Giants." Unfortunately, the magazine went to press July 15, 1994, the very day Phil Simms was cut from the Giants.

SMART MOUTH?

Joe Theismann was a star quarterback for the Washington Redskins during his NFL playing days, but he didn't always make the right call off the field. In 1993, Joe said, "The word genius isn't applicable in football. A genius is a guy like Norman Einstein." Norman? Perhaps Joe meant Albert Einstein, the world-famous physicist.

HANDS-DOWN PLAYING

New York Jets quarterback Richard Todd came up with a new way to respond to the fans who booed him during a game at Shea Stadium in 1979. Todd gave the fans a two-arms-up, one-finger-up salute. Richard Todd later regretted his digital display, and publicly apologized for losing his cool.

AIR BALL

In 1978, Oakland Raiders quarterback Ken Stabler refused to grant interviews to sports reporters. Stabler said his passing would do his talking for him. It was a good thing Kenny kept silent that season, because he was intercepted 30 times in 1978.

SMART CALL?

Hall of Fame quarterback Johnny Unitas, who passed for 40,239 yards and 290 touchdowns in 18 NFL seasons, was cut by the Pittsburgh Steelers during his rookie season. Unitas was axed without ever playing a single exhibition game for Pittsburgh. A Steelers coach said Johnny was too dumb to play pro football. Guess who turned out to be the real dummy?

BRAWN OR BRAINS?

In 1989, top quarterbacks Troy Aikman and Steve Walsh were competing for the starting job with the Dallas Cowboys. Quarterback coach Jerry Rhome was asked to compare the two. Rhome said, "If you sat down to build an NFL quarterback, Troy is what you'd come up with. He's 6 feet, three inchs tall, 220 pounds, has great arm speed—everything is perfect."

Then Rhome touted Walsh's pulses. "And Steve?" he said. "I like his mind!"

BALD TRUTH

Joe Namath, quarterback for the New York Jets, was one of pro football's first long-haired stars. Namath was so famous for his long locks, he poked fun at himself in his autobiography.

"I arrived in Beaver Falls (Pa.) for the first time, May 13, 1943," Joe wrote about his birth. "I wore my hair short then."

NOT FUMBLING FOR WORDS

PINK WORD SLIP

Green Bay Packers head coach Vince Lombardi once told his troops, "If you aren't fired with enthusiasm, you'll be fired with enthusiasm."

SEE YA!

Fred Arbanas was an All-Pro tight end who played for the Kansas City Chiefs in the 1960s. Arbanas had one glass eye that never seemed to inhibit his ability to catch passes. Referee Tom Bell, who had great admiration for Fred, once asked Arbanas what he'd do if his other eye were ever injured. Said Fred Arbanas to Tom Bell with a straight face, "I'd become a referee just like you."

NOT A FALL GUY

When Buddy Ryan was head coach of the Philadelphia Eagles, most of his players were totally devoted to him. Defensive tackle Jerome Brown's devotion was not so extreme. "If Buddy told me to jump off a bridge," he said, "well, I could do it, but I'd think about it."

QUITE A CHARACTER

When Ray Malavasi was the head coach of the Los Angeles Rams, he sensed that winning was everything in his sport. "They say losing builds character," said coach Malavasi. "I have all the character I need."

BRAINY BOOTER

Punter Pat McInally of the Cincinnati Bengals was a bit of a gridiron guru. He once quipped, "At Harvard, they labeled me a jock. In the pros, they consider me an intellectual."

OKAY, ACE

In 1991, All-Pro linebacker Lawrence Taylor showed up six hours late for the first day of the New York Giants' training camp. "Don't blame me," Taylor said as he explained why he was slow in arriving. "Blame the foursome in front of me."

WHAT'S COOKING?

When coach Bill Parcells was hired by the New York Jets in 1977, he wanted to be certain he'd have complete control of his new gridiron squad. Parcells tactfully explained his need for total power to the press. "If they want you to cook the dinner," said Parcells, "at least they ought to let you shop for some of the groceries."

WINDOW DRESSING

Detroit Lions coach Monte Clark once described how tough Miami Dolphins running back Larry Csonka was. "When he goes on safari," Clark explained, "the lions roll up their windows."

DON'T INTERFERE

Pittsburgh Steelers defensive back Willie Williams was called for pass interference against Houston Oilers receiver Chris Sanders in an NFL contest in 1996. Williams didn't contest the call. He just shrugged his shoulders and said, "I'd rather move the sticks then give up six."

BUMMED OUT

After quitting pro football, former NFL head coach Bum Phillips was asked how his retirement was going. "I ain't doing a damn thing," said Bum, "and I don't start until noon."

COLD SUPPER

The Chicago Bears played an exhibition football game in Germany in the early 1990s. On the Bears' squad at the time was 300-pound-plus defensive lineman William "Refrigerator" Perry. After watching Perry perform on the gridiron, a German football fan stated, "That number seventy-two is unbelievable. He's eaten many hamburgers!"

TOUGH GUY

Defensive end Willie Davis of the Green Bay Packers had so

many tackles in a game against the Minnesota Vikings in 1996 that Detroit Lions coach Harry Gilmer, who was watching the contest, said, "Willie Davis is a one-man gang!"

COURTING FAILURE

The United States Football League tried to compete against the National Football League in 1986, but failed to draw enough fans to survive. At one point during the league wars, the USFL filed an antitrust suit against the NFL, which prompted comedian David Letterman to comment, "There were 150 people in the courtroom—the third largest crowd to ever see the USFL in action."

SHOW ME

Terry Bradshaw, the former Pittsburgh Steelers quarterback, was working as an NFL analyst when he offered viewers some passing advice. "If a receiver is open, throw it to him," suggested Bradshaw. "If he's not open, throw it to him anyway. Let the guy show his athletic ability."

GAME PLAYER

Head coach Hank Stram of the Kansas City Chiefs was talking about the sport of football. "It's only a game when you win," said Hank. "When you lose, it's hell."

RUN FOR YOUR LIFE

In 1974, the Houston Oilers had an anemic running game.

John Breen, General Manager of the Oilers, described Houston's ground attack this way. "We were tipping off our running plays," Breen joked. "Whenever we broke from the huddle, three backs were laughing and one was pale as a ghost."

THE PAYOFF

Dick Vermeil, the former coach of the Philadelphia Eagles, disagreed with NFL coaches who admitted they didn't expect their players to get up for every game during a long season. "I don't believe in this business of players being way up one week and way down the next," Vermeil said. "Hey! When a player goes in to pick up his paycheck on Monday, it's the same size it was the Monday before."

TAKE A CHANCE

NFL coach George Allen was once asked if hard work or pure luck produced more football victories. "The harder I work, the luckier I get," answered Allen.

MONEY MAN

The Chicago Bears paid middle linebacker Dick Butkus the reported sum of $200,000 in salary and bonus to sign with their team in 1964. At the time, the $200,000 was a record amount. Team owner George Halas, a man not known for his generosity, had this to say about the sum: "We gave Butkus more money than we used to pay the entire team a few years ago," complained Halas.

BIG SPENDER

Former Chicago Bears coach Mike Ditka (who coached the Bears for eleven seasons) said this about team owner

George Halas' aversion to spending money: "He tosses nickels around like they're manhole covers."

MOM'S DISMAY

NFL linebacker Brian Bosworth of the Seattle Seahawks was a bit of a wild child, according to his mom. Brian's mother once said, "It's a good thing Brian was a third child or he would have been an only one."

GROWTH PROBLEM

Gary Jeter, who played defensive end for the New York Jets in the 1980s, was asked how he became a pro football player. "I liked baseball more," Jetter admitted, "but instead of growing up, I grew out."

MOMMA'S BOY

Minnesota Vikings coach Bud Grant had Leo Lewis on his team in the 1980s. Lewis was a good receiver, but he was frequently too injured to play. One day, Grant was chatting with reporters about his injury-plagued receiver. "I told Leo I coached his father in Canada," said Grant. "He never missed a game in ten years. I guess Leo took after his mother."

OUCH!

Middle linebacker Dick Butkus was known for his ferocity as a player. "I wouldn't ever set out to hurt anybody deliberately," said Butkus, "unless it was important—like a league game or something."

SKINHEAD

Reporters got a good laugh when they teased Detroit Lions

linebacker Wayne Walker about being bald. "Somewhere in Detroit," said Walker, "there's a helmet with all my hair in it."

CASH FLOW

Los Angeles Rams quarterback Art Hayden was duly impressed when he saw million-dollar-rookie Johnny Johnson return a interception 99 yards for a touchdown in the 1980s." His big wallet didn't slow him down," remarked Hayden about Johnson's scoring scamper.

THINK ABOUT IT

"Everyone has some fear," coach Walt Michaels of the New York Jets once said. "A man who has no fear belongs in a mental institution...or on special teams."

CATCH PHRASE

Pro football Hall of Fame receiver Ray Berry was the receivers' coach for the New England Patriots in 1979. Despite Berry's tutelage, the receivers had a tough time hauling in passes that year and dropped too many catchable balls. When head coach Ron Erhardt was questioned about Ray Berry's apparent failure to improve the catching ability of the Patriots' receivers, Erhardt replied, "Raymond is coaching them—not catching them."

NEEDY PERSON

"A good coach needs a patient wife, a loyal dog, and a great quarterback," head coach Bud Grant of the Minnesota Vikings once said to reporters. After a short pause, Grant added, "and not necessarily in that order."

BAD BOY

Tampa Bay Buccaneers offensive guard Jim Leonard once told reporters about his mom, who ran two homes for delinquents. "I helped her get ready for her job."

KICK HIM OUT

Garo Yepremian was the first soccer-style kicker to make it big in the National Football League. Yepremian was a Cypriot (from the island of Cyprus in the eastern Mediterranean) who became a member of the Detriot Lions in 1966. In his first NFL season, Garo set a record by booting six field goals in a single game. When a sports reporter asked an opposing NFL coach the best way to stop Yepremian, he promptly replied, "Tighten the immigration laws!"

BIG TALK

Gene Upshaw played offensive guard and Art Shell played offensive tackle for the Oakland Raiders in the late 1960s. Upshaw and Shell were so big and strong, Doug Sutherland, a defensive tackle for the Minnesota Vikings, paid the duo this compliment. "They could block out the sun," Sutherland quipped.

WORK OF ART

Some people thought Walter Payton of the Chicago Bears was born to be a professional NFL running back. When Bears backfield coach Fred O'Connor saw Payton in the locker room for the first time, he marveled, "I thought God must have taken a chisel and said, 'I gonna make me a halfback!'"

NUMBER, PLEASE

A football reporter once said, "NFL players who claim they always give 110% on the field obviously didn't major in math at college."

HELLO, AGAIN

After a thirteen-year NFL career, linebacker Kyle Clifton of the New York Jets retired from pro football in 1995. His teammates tossed him a farewell retirement luncheon to mark the occasion. However, Clifton promptly had a change of heart. Kyle showed up at the Jets' mini-camp the next season and made the squad. At the end of the 1996 season, Kyle Clifton decided to retire again. And once again, Clifton's teammates held another farewell luncheon for him. "This is the Second Annual Farewell Party," announced teammate Marvin Washington. Then he added, "And it's the last one we're giving him."

HUMBLE GUY

Safety Tim Foley of the Miami Dolphins once said, "Humility is always one play away."

TASTEFUL REPLY

NFL running back Hershel Walker is a die-hard teetotaler. He doesn't touch alcohol. Someone once asked him if he wasn't curious about trying a drink. "I'm curious about jumping off a cliff," replied Walker, "and I don't do that either."

IN YOUR FACE

Sports broadcaster Howard Cosell, who won fame as a member of the Monday Night Football broadcast team, once asked *New York Times* sports columnist Red Smith how many great television sports broadcasters there were. Smith smirked and answered, "One less than you think."

WHAT A LAUGH!

Playing in the NFL wasn't as tough as being on a gridiron squad when comedian Rodney Dangerfield went to school. According to Dangerfield, "Our school was so tough that in our football games after they sacked the quarterback, they went after his family."

THE GOOFY GRIDIRON

FAR OUT

ABC's Monday Night Football broadcast team was covering an Oakland Raiders game when the television camera zoomed in on a Raiders defensive lineman with a shaved head and menacing manner. "That's Otis Sistrunk," said announcer Alex Karras, introducing Sistrunk, who had not played college football but had graduated to the NFL from a minor-league team called the Norfolk Neptunes. "He's from the University of Mars."

INJURY-FREE FALL

Jim Marshall was an All-Pro defensive lineman for the Minnesota Vikings. One of Marshall's many astonishing feats on the gridiron during his 20-year career was starting 282 consecutive NFL games. To start that many pro contests, a player must stay injury-free. In 1979, Jim Marshall retired from the violent world of pro football to pursue his hobbies, one of which was hang gliding. Strangely enough, Jim suffered his first serious injury on August 12, 1980, when his hang glider crashed into a light pole on a high-school football field.

LOOK-IN PASS

In the 1930's, when Sammy Baugh was playing quarterback for the Washington Redskins, pro football players wore helmets that did not have face masks on them. One day early in Baugh's career, a big defensive tackle from an opposing team

kept hitting Sammy in the face every chance he got. On one play, the tackle smacked Baugh in the nose with his forearm. On another play, he slammed his fist into Sam's eyes.

"Knock it off," Sammy Baugh told the opposing tackle. When the defender refused to quit battering the Washington quarterback, Sammy Baugh got revenge his own way. Baugh told his offensive lineman not to block the tackle on a particular pass play. When the ball was snapped, the big tackle rushed right at Sammy Baugh. The Washington quarterback took aim and fired a bullet of a pass right into the tackle's face. The ball hit the defender and knocked him out. He was carried out of the game on a stretcher.

DON'T FLIP OUT

Art Rooney, the owner of the Pittsburgh Steelers, had a strange theory about the coin toss at the start of a football game. Rooney stressed that one should never call the coin toss, but should instead defer the call to the other football team. He believed that making your opponent choose heads or tails puts undue pressure on him to make the right call.

LOSERS DO WIN!

Only the best teams are supposed to make the play-offs, right? Wrong. In 1981, the Montreal Alouettes of the Canadian Football League made the CFL's Eastern Division play-offs with a record of 3 wins and 13 losses. The Ottawa Rough Riders finished ahead of the Alouettes with a record of 5 wins and 11 losses. To make the division play-offs, Montreal edged the Toronto Argonauts, who finished last with a record of 2–14!

DEAD END

A popular rumor concerning Giants Stadium at the Meadowlands in East Rutherford, New Jersey, is that former union leader Jimmy Hoffa is buried underneath the stadium. The rumor persists because Jimmy Hoffa vanished in 1975, the year the stadium was constructed, and has never been found. However, no evidence of a body was discovered in 1989 when Giants Stadium underwent massive reconstruction. Nevertheless, the old rumor later prompted New York punter Sean Landeta to come up with a bit of dark humor concerning the Hoffa stadium story. Said Landeta, "I guess it gives meaning to the phrase 'kicking into the coffin corner.'"

PAYBACK

When Norm Van Brocklin was quarterback for the Los Angeles Rams in the 1950s, a season-ticket form was mailed to him by mistake. Van Brocklin returned the form like any faithful Rams fan would do, and in the box reserved for suggestions Norm wrote, "Pay Van Brocklin a million dollars."

GROUNDED EAGLE

Fullback Bronko Nagurski of the Chicago Bears greeted Philadelphia Eagles linebacker John "Bull" Lipski in typical Nagurski fashion in a 1933 gridiron contest. Bronko knocked Bull unconscious three times in the same game.

BANG-UP ENDING

In 1958, a Baltimore Colts fan was listening to the NFL championship game between the Colts and the New York Giants while driving his car. When Colts placekicker Steve Myhra kicked a game-tying field goal late in the fourth quarter, the Baltimore fan became so excited that he lost control

of his car and crashed into a telephone pole. Luckily, the fan wasn't injured. Even luckier, the Colts won the NFL title in overtime.

SAINTS BE PRAISED

Halfback Paul Hornung of the Green Bay Packers told this story about his egotistical coach, Vince Lombardi. One chilly night Vince came home after practice and got into bed with his wife. "God," exclaimed Mrs. Lombardi, "are your feet cold!"

"I know," replied her husband, "but around the house you can call me Vince."

GROUNDED

It was bad enough when the New Orleans Saints traveled to Pittsburgh in 1993 and were whipped 37–14 by the Steelers. Nevertheless, the Saints' troubles did not end after the lopsided loss. When the Saints squad boarded a jet for the flight home, a small motor on the left wing of the plane exploded as it taxied down the runway. The squad's journey back to New Orleans was delayed another two and one-half hours.

BOYHOOD DREAM

In 1965, the NFL granted a team franchise to the Atlanta Falcons. The group that owned the Falcons was headed by Rankin McEachern Smith, an insurance executive and a life-long sports fan. When reporters asked why Smith had purchased a pro football franchise, Smith looked surprised and answered, "I thought every red-blooded American boy wanted to grow up to own a pro football team," he said.

THE DEEP SIX

In 1996, the New York Jets and the Oakland Raiders both suf-

36

fered through dismal NFL seasons. When the two teams met to play each other, a headline in the *New York Post* described the matchup in this way: "Sinking Ships Collide!"

ACCIDENTALLY ON PURPOSE

Tackle Joe Stydahar was a tough guy with a nice personality. Stydahar played for the Chicago Bears during the late 1930s. In a game against the New York Giants in 1938, he faced off against Giant rookie end Will Walls. At the snap of the ball, Stydahar fired across the line of scrimmage and smashed Walls in the face with a forearm. The blow stunned Walls and knocked him back onto the seat of his pants. After the whistle blew, Joe Stydahar bent over Walls and helped the dazed rookie get to his feet.

"I didn't mean to do that, kid," Stydahar said politely as he patted Will on the back. "You've got to believe me. I was just excited. It won't happen again."

The two men went back to their respective huddles. On the next snap of the ball, Stydahar again fired across the line and whacked Will Walls in the face with a forearm shot that sent the rookie sailing backwards. As Walls slowly got to his feet, Stydahar smiled at him and said, "Son, you've got to stay alert in this league."

THE BEST MAN

General Manager Cal Murphy of the Canadian Football League's Winnipeg Blue Bombers found his team without a head coach in April 1992. It was Murphy's job to find the best man to fill the vacancy. After considering who to hire for several weeks, Murphy decided on a guy he believed had the best qualifications for the position–he named *himself* the new head coach of the Winnipeg Blue Bombers. The choice wasn't that much of a surprise. Cal Murphy had led the Blue Bombers to the CFL Championship back in 1984.

CHILL FACTOR

The Philadelphia Eagles defeated the Chicago Cardinals 7–0 in the 1948 NFL Championship game. The contest was really for the birds because it was played in a howling blizzard.

PIGSKIN POWER

The power of professional football in America is a bit shocking. In 1980, the League of Women Voters rescheduled a presidential debate to avoid a conflict with an ABC Monday Night Football broadcast.

THANKS FOR THE PAY

In the early 1960s, the St. Louis Cardinals made big defensive tackle Harold Lucas of Michigan State their second-round draft pick. Harold was paid a hefty $250,000 signing bonus. When the six-foot, two-inch Lucas arrived at the Cardinals' training camp, coaches were astonished to see that he weighed around 365 pounds! The coaches blasted Harold for being overweight. Day after day they yelled and screamed at Lucas, trying to bully him into losing weight.

Harold was a sensitive individual. Finally, a week later he'd had enough. He packed his belongings and left. Since the Cardinals' executive who negotiated Lucas' contract had forgotten to include a clause about training camp, Harold got to keep his signing bonus. Harold Lucas received a quarter of a million dollars for a pro football trial that lasted just one week.

TOUGH TRYOUT

Making the roster of the Washington Redskins in 1989 was really tough for free-agent players. Due to a rule which stated that a NFL squad could not have more than 80 players under contract after June 1, the Redskins were forced to cut three free agents from the team roster before the players even had a chance to put on their pads in training camp.

BROWNOUT

The Cleveland Browns moved to Baltimore to become the Baltimore Ravens in the mid-1990s. Before the franchise moved, the Browns suffered through some tough losing seasons in Cleveland. In 1990, when the Browns were 3–13, Cleveland fans started to blame team owner Art Modell for the downfall of the Browns' squad. One fan banner displayed at Cleveland's Municipal Stadium read, "Expression is a form of art. Losing is a work of Art!"

BID ME FAREWELL

Fullback Willie Heston of the University of Michigan had professional football teams hungering for his services in the early 1900s. Heston refused to turn pro unless he received a lot of money. He told representatives of the Canton Bulldogs, the Chicago Tigers, and other pro teams that he was auctioning off his football talents to the professional squad that bid the highest for his services. The early pro teams refused to get into a bidding war over him, so Heston never played professional ball. Willie Heston could well be professional football's first holdout.

SOCK HOP

In 1980, linebacker Reggie Williams of the Cincinnati Bengals was socked with a $1,000 fine because his uniform did not conform with the NFL dress code. What was the big infraction? Reggie's knee socks weren't taped up, and they dropped down to his ankles during play against the Houston Oilers.

GAME TALK

"Football is blocking and tackling," said Green Bay Packers coach Vince Lombardi. "Everything else is mythology."

SIGNING OFF

In 1980, two young women who were hippies went up to Pittsburgh Steelers linebacker Jack Lambert to ask him an important question. "What's your astrological sign?" the women want to know.

"Feces," replied Jack Lambert.

FIRE POWER

A sports reporter once said, "There are two kinds of pro foot-ball teams—those that wish they had fired their coach last fall and those that wish they hadn't!"

FLY GUY

When Errol Mann, a veteran kicker in the NFL, signed to play with the Oakland Raiders, he flew to training camp in his own airplane. Mann, who had just received his pilot's license, offered to take Raiders quarterback Ken Stabler up for a ride after practice. Stabler quickly refused to fly with the NFL placekicker.

"No offense, Errol," said Kenny, "but all of your skills lie in your feet. You really should have taken up tap dancing instead of flying."

FUNNY MONEY

Who says NFL owners don't have a sense of humor? After an NFL team lost a close game to an arch-rival, the head coach tried to explain the cause of the defeat to the team owner. "It was the play of the defensive line," said the coach. "Those guys didn't charge enough."

"Are you kidding?" snapped the owner. "Those four guys are already charging more than I can afford to pay them."

GIVE 'EM A HAND

A Monday Night Football game between the Oakland Raiders and the Houston Oilers turned out to be a boring blowout. The game was so horrible that television director Dennis Lewin instructed his cameramen to pan the stands to look for interesting shots to spice up the broadcast. When Lewin spotted a bored fan dozing in a deserted part of the stadium, the director ordered the cameraman to zoom in for a close-up. As soon as the cameraman established the shot on the snoozing fan, it was broadcast live. The disgruntled fan suddenly awoke and flashed the cameraman an obscene gesture, holding up his middle finger. Everyone in the television broadcast booth gasped. "Hey! That just means we're number one!" Dennis Lewin said into the off-air microphone with which he spoke to the game announcers. In the broadcast booth, game analyst Don Meredith repeated Lewin's quip on the air to the football fans, and a nasty incident was turned into one of pro football's funniest moments.

RAW POWER

Offensive lineman Bob St. Clair, who played for the San Francisco 49ers in the 1950s and 1960s, enjoyed eating *raw* beefsteak!

COLD FRONT

The Denver Broncos suffered through a four-game losing streak in 1994, but were not abandoned by most of their fans. Two Bronco fans, Daren Trapp and Walt Dalton, gave Denver the cold shoulder, but in a positive way. Trapp and Dalton announced they would sit on the roof of a Colorado bar no matter what the weather was like until Denver won an NFL football contest. The two Denver diehards braved icy rain and chilling winds for five days until Denver finally defeated the Seattle Seahawks 16–9 on October 9, 1994.

FOOTBALL ANIMALS

Early in quarterback Frank Ryan's career with the Cleveland Browns, which lasted from 1962 to 1968, he was often criticized by fans and sportswriters. One afternoon, Frank took his children to the Cleveland zoo. The next day a teammate asked Ryan about the trip. "It was wonderful," said Frank Ryan. "The animals must be the only group in Cleveland that is not criticizing me."

IT'S A JUNGLE

Los Angeles Rams line coach Don Paul once described pro football the following way: "It's game played for pay by huge, finely trained animals," said Paul.

ANONYMOUS FANS

The New Orleans Saints were cursed in 1980. The team lost its first 12 games that season. Prior to that year, the Saints had never posted a better than 500 record in their 14-year NFL history. However, it was in 1980 that the New Orleans fans finally started to lose hope. They were so embarrassed about their team's record that they began to show up at home games wearing brown paper bags over their heads so they would not be recognized as Saints fans.

BETTER LATE THAN NEVER

Pittsburgh Steelers defensive lineman "Mean" Joe Greene was featured on the cover of *Sports Illustrated* magazine for the October 11, 1971, issue. Pete and Bonnie Kincaid of Columbus, Ohio, subscribed to *Sports Illustrated* for their son Danny in the 1970s, but never had a chance to scan the issue featuring Mean Joe. The magazine did not arrive at the Kincaid home until almost 24 years later. The October 11, 1971, issue of *Sports Illustrated* was finally delivered to Pete and Bonnie in 1995.

WHICH TEAM ARE YOU ON?

In the early 1900s, pro football players did not sign binding contracts with the teams for which they played. Good players often jumped from team to team during a season, playing for the pro squad that offered them the most money. It is rumored that in the 1916 season young end Knute Rockne played for six different teams.

TRICK OR TREAT

Linebacker Ted Hendricks of the Oakland Raiders did some crazy things during his NFL career, which lasted from 1969 to 1983. Once he showed up for practice on Halloween wearing a hollowed-out pumpkin as a helmet.

LOOK OUT BELOW

In 1978, a New Orleans Saints fan was so upset over a call made by the referee that he threw his binoculars at the ref from the second tier of the Superdome. The fan quickly learned to contain his temper in the future. Instead of the referee, he hit a policeman with his binoculars.

LUCKY CHARM

In 1982, farmers in Boise, Idaho, were plagued by thousands of wild rabbits that threatened to destroy potential crops. The farmers banded together to plan a massive rabbit hunt. Luckily for the rabbits, the hunt, which was planned for a Sunday in the month of January, had to be postponed. The farmers made the mistake of scheduling the big rabbit hunt on the same day of the Super Bowl and decided to watch the game instead.

KICKS AND BUCKS

The NFL's best placekickers had a hard time splitting the uprights at the 1997 Pro Bowl. Cary Blanchard, the AFC's (American Football Conference's) All-Pro kicker from the Indianapolis Colts, and John Kasay, the NFC's (National Football Conference's) All-Pro booter from the Carolina Panthers, combined for a 3 of 8 performance. The AFC won the game 26–23 thanks to a 37-yard kick by Blanchard in overtime.

However, kicking honors at the Bowl went to Lance Alstodt, an investment banker. Alstodt got one chance to make a 35-yard field goal at halftime. Lance drilled the kick and collected a cool one million dollars in prize money for his feat. The promotion was the climax of a nationwide contest. Isn't it amazing what an amateur can accomplish with a little incentive?

BIG BROTHER IS WATCHING

NFL officials have an "observer" at all pro games. It is the job of the observer to note whether players' shirts are tucked in, their socks are aligned, and the correct shoes are being worn (only a certain number of players can wear shoes other than the league-certified brand).

BAD EXAMPLE

Pro football can have a bad influence on good people. Sometimes even the best of people are the worst fans. In 1995, 175 people were ejected from the stands at Giants Stadium for rowdy behavior. Those ejected included a prominent teacher and a police chief!

WHEEL FUNNY

The Cleveland Browns' performance during the 1978 NFL season was such a series of up-and-down games that the teams' highlight film at the end of the year was dubbed "A Rollercoaster Ride."

NAMELESS

On July 7, 1994, Baltimore beat the Toronto Argonauts 28–20 in a Canadian Football League game. Baltimore, a first-year CFL team, played the contest without an official team nickname. Baltimore wanted to use the name "Colts," but the NFL's Indianapolis Colts (which moved to Indianapolis from Baltimore) secured a court injunction that prevented the new Baltimore team from doing so. But what's in a name? What's important is whether you win the game.

DAFFY DEFENDERS

HIT PARADE

Tommy Nobis of the Atlanta Falcons was one of the NFL's greatest linebackers. In his rookie season, Nobis was playing middle linebacker against the Philadelphia Eagles when the Eagles' 275-pound offensive tackle Bob Brown came out of nowhere and crushed Tommy with a block that sent him flying. After the game, Tommy Nobis talked about the great job Brown did on that block with former Eagles player Tom Brookshier. "I saw it," Brookshier told Nobis. "Getting hit that way is like walking along a street and having a truck fall on you."

A KEEPER

Defensive tackle Eugene "Big Daddy" Lipscomb, who played for the Baltimore Colts and the Pittsburgh Steelers, was asked by reporters how he always managed to make so many tackles. Lipscomb explained his ability this way: "I just wrap my arms around the whole backfield and peel them off until I get to the ballcarrier. Him...I keep!"

SAY IT AIN'T SLOW

At six feet, five inches tall and 225 pounds, defensive end David "Deacon" Jones of the Los Angeles Rams was big, tough, and fast. Deacon's speed on the football field not only surprised but often shocked opposing offensive players. Once, speedy halfback Mark Woodson of the Pittsburgh Steelers took a handoff and broke into the open. He sprinted down the sideline, thinking he was about to score a touchdown. Suddenly, he was tackled from behind by a Rams player. "Oh, no," Woodson yelled before he saw who had caught him. "Say it's not you!"

"It's me! It's me!" Deacon Jones hollered to Woodson. "It's the only man who could catch you."

Another time, fleet pass receiver Bobby Mitchell of the Cleveland Browns snared a pass and turned upfield. Deacon Jones pursued him from an angle and could have easily made the tackle. Instead, Deacon ran beside Bobby for about five yards before knocking the swift receiver out of bounds. "Why didn't you tackle him right away?" the Rams' head coach asked Jones when he came off the field.

"Sorry, coach," Deacon apologized, "but I just had to find out if I was as fast as Mitchell—and I was!"

LEAP OF FAITH

Baltimore Colts Hall-of-Famer Gino Marchetti was one of the quickest defensive ends to ever play in the NFL, and one of the most difficult pass rushers to block. One day in training camp, Marchetti was going against a rookie lineman who just couldn't block him. Marchetti went around the rookie from the right side and then from the left side. Finally, the offensive line coach gave the new player some advice. "To block Marchetti you have to get lower in your stance," the coach said. The rookie listened to the advice and nodded.

On the next play, the rookie stayed low as the ball was snapped. Marchetti put one hand on the rookie's helmet, jumped over the blocker, and raced into the backfield to make the play.

"What do I do now?" the disgusted rookie asked the offensive coach.

Art Donovan, the star defensive tackle who played on the line with Gino Marchetti, had the answer. "If I were you, kid," Donovan called out, "I'd applaud!"

REVERSE RUN

It is the dream of every defensive player to steal the ball and race for a touchdown. Sometimes dreams do come true. Defensive end Jim Marshall of the Minnesota Vikings saw his dream play materialize in a game against the San Francisco 49ers in 1961. Marshall scooped up a fumble, spun around, and broke into the clear. Jim headed for the goal line, and it was then that his dream turned into a nightmare. He had run the wrong way. As his teammates screamed for him to run in the opposite direction, Jim Marshall rumbled 60 yards with the ball and dashed into the opposing team's end zone, where he was tackled by a San Francisco player. Instead of scoring a touchdown for the Vikings, Jim Marshall scored a safety for the 49ers. Luckily, Jim's goof didn't affect the outcome of the NFL contest as Minnesota eventually defeated San Francisco 27–22. Nevertheless, the strange play was a dream gone haywire!

FISH OR FOWL?

Tampa Bay Buccaneers defensive tackle Dave Stalls was a man with some strange hobbies. When he didn't feel very brave, his hobby was bird-watching. When he did feel brave, his hobby was doing shark research.

JUST A NIBBLE

In 1960, the Green Bay Packers squared off against the Los Angeles Rams in an NFL contest. During the game, Rams linebacker Les Richter leveled the Packers' rugged fullback Jim Taylor. Taylor was so angry that during the pileup he bit one of Richter's fingers. Les Richter jumped up and ran over to the referee. He demanded that the ref hit the Packers with a 15-yard penalty for roughness.

"I see teeth marks, but no blood," said the ref. "No penalty."

The linebacker stormed away from the ref. "Hey, Taylor," Les Richter yelled to the fullback, who was in the Green Bay huddle. "The next time bite it clean off. We need the yardage!"

NOT A BIRDBRAIN

In his playing days with the Philadelphia Eagles, defensive star Tim Rossovich was known to be a bit zany. Once during a team meeting, Rossovich silently walked into a room and sat down. His quiet behavior puzzled his teammates until wacky Tim Rossovich finally opened his mouth. Out flew a tiny sparrow which circled above the heads of the astonished Eagle players.

MONEY GAME

Everyone knows money is a key factor in the NFL. Defensive back Emlen Tunnell was aware of that fact back in 1953 when

he was a member of the New York Giants. When the Giants played the Los Angeles Rams that season, the defense had trouble tackling the Rams' star-runner-turned-receiver Elroy "Crazy Legs" Hirsch. After Hirsch snared a pass and ran by Tunnell to tally a Rams touchdown, Giants coach Steve Owen cornered Emlen Tunnell on the sidelines. "Why did you let Hirsch get by you?" Owen screamed.

"Hey, coach," answered Emlen. "I get paid $8,000 a year and Hirsch gets paid $18,000 a year. He's supposed to get by me!"

OLD-TIMER

Linebacker Lee Roy Jordan was 35 years old when his Dallas Cowboys team played in Super Bowl X in 1976, against the Pittsburgh Steelers. Before the big game, Jordan stood on the sidelines of the practice field and watched his much younger teammates work out. It made Lee Roy sense just how old he really was for an NFL player. "I feel like the scout master at a Boy Scout jamboree," Lee Roy told the reporters standing near him. By the way, the Cowboys lost to the Pittsburgh Steelers 21–17.

NO EXCUSES

NFL defensive lineman Mike Reid didn't care for failure. "There are a thousand reasons for failure," Reid once said, "but not a single excuse."

TIMBER!

The St. Louis Cardinals' Larry Wilson had a reputation as a hard hitter during his playing days. Wilson, who was a safety, often knocked people flying. However, in a contest against the Cleveland Browns, Cleveland halfback Ernie Green turned the tables on Larry Wilson. The Cardinals' safety tried to blitz the Browns' quarterback, but a savage block by Green leveled him. "When we watched the game films of that block," Wilson later said, "I looked like a big tree falling."

NOT LETTER PERFECT

Thomas "Hollywood" Henderson got his nickname because of his flamboyant ways on and off the field. The Dallas Cowboys' linebacker also had very little respect for opposing quarterbacks during his playing days. Hollywood once had this to say about Pittsburgh Steelers All-Star quarterback Terry Bradshaw's intelligence. "Bradshaw," quipped Henderson, "couldn't spell cat if you spotted him the C and the A!"

BAGGED

Defensive lineman David "Deacon" Jones was inducted into the Pro Football Hall of Fame in 1980. Jones is credited with coming up with the gridiron term "sack" to describe tackling the opposing quarterback for a loss while he attempts to pass. When asked how he came up with the word "sack," Jones offered this explanation: "Like you know, you sack a city," Jones said. "You devastate it."

DIAL 911!

Middle linebacker Sam Huff, who played for the New York Giants and the Washington Redskins, was asked what it was like to tackle the great Cleveland Browns running back Jim Brown. "All you can do is grab hold," Huff explained, "and hang on and wait for help."

LOONY LINEMEN

DARN DARWIN

In the mid-1980s, Bob Golic of the Cleveland Browns was forced to make a drastic position transition. Golic was switched from linebacker to nose tackle. "I pretty much describe the transition as Darwin's Theory of Re-Evolution," Golic explained to reporters. "I'm going from a walking, thinking, upright human being on two legs to a crawling, groveling, sniveling four-legged beast of burden."

Bob Golic was later asked when he finally realized he'd make it as a pro defensive lineman. Bob stated it occurred to him during a pass rush situation. "As I came toward the quarterback," said Bob, "I saw an offensive lineman waiting for me. I put my head down and rammed into him." Golic then smiled and continued. "At that point I believe the brain cells started dying and I started making the conversion to nose tackle."

DOWN THE DRAIN

John Matuszak of the Oakland Raiders was a big defensive end. Matuszak once demonstrated his strength to his teammates by yanking a toilet out of the floor in a hotel bathroom. His teammates were so shocked that they flushed (red) in surprise.

A ROSE BY ANY OTHER NAME

Fullback Jim Brown and defensive tackle Bob Lilly are both in the Pro Football Hall of Fame. When Brown was a fullback for the Cleveland Browns, he bumped heads with Lilly, who was playing for the Dallas Cowboys, in a game in 1964. After the contest, a reporter asked Jim Brown about Bob Lilly. "He hits hard," said Jim as he smiled. "A lot harder than a lily. He's more like a thorn."

THE ANSWER MAN

Ray Mansfield, a veteran player on the Pittsburgh Steelers team that won Super Bowls in 1994 and 1995, was never bothered by persistent reporters seeking interviews. "I can't understand why players complain about the press bothering them so much," said Mansfield. "For ten years nobody asked me a question."

I SEE THE LIGHT

Baltimore Colts defensive tackle Art Donovan battled weight problems throughout his NFL career. Art was always over-weight. "I'm a light eater," Donovan once said. "I start eating when it gets light."

BIG TALK

In 1996, the Dallas Cowboys were beating the Pittsburgh Steelers and running out the clock when Steelers linebacker Kevin Greene let his rage over the upcoming loss spill out. He shouted to the Dallas offense, "Hey! You couldn't run the ball on us. We shut down that great running game."

Kevin's comments ticked off the Cowboys' offensive line-men. Dallas guard Nate Newton had the perfect comeback to Greene's outburst. "Look at the scoreboard," he shouted to the Pittsburgh linebacker. "Last time I checked, the team with the most points wins."

TEACH THEM A LESSON

Defensive lineman Merlin Olsen enjoyed a very successful career with the Los Angeles Rams. It is ironic that his ninth-grade gridiron coach urged him to give up football. "What are you trying to do to yourself?" the coach told Merlin. "You should use your energy for something else like the school paper."

But Olsen disregarded this advice and continued to play football. Eventually, he played in 14 NFL Pro Bowls and was elected to the NFL Hall of Fame. Whatever became of his ninth-grade football coach, no one knows.

WE TOLD YOUR MOM

Lester Holmes, a 305-pound offensive lineman, was the top pick of the Philadelphia Eagles in the 1993 NFL draft. When Holmes refused to sign a contract with the Eagles and skipped rookie training camp, Philadelphia took drastic measures. The Eagles sent a letter to Gertrude Holmes, Lester's 65-year-old mom, stating that her son was making a big mistake by not joining the team. Lester Holmes intercepted the letter before his mom could read it. "I was humiliated!" Lester told reporters as he explained about the letter from the pro team that had drafted him. "I don't think my mom should have been brought into this."

WAVE GOODBYE

Offensive tackle Russ Washington played for the San Diego Chargers during the 1970s. Russ enjoyed his privacy during the off-season, and was a hard man to find when he wasn't playing football. Russ Washington's off-season home was a grass hut on a small island in the Pacific Ocean!

RACE DISGRACE

Coach Weeb Ewbank of the Baltimore Colts utilized defensive tackle Art Donovan in many different ways. Donovan was a key figure in many defensive schemes the Colts used. Art was also so slow that coach Ewbank used his big tackle to test potential Colt rookies. Weeb Ewbank made would-be Baltimore players race against him. If Donovan won the race, coach Ewbank knew the rookie was too slow to play in the NFL and axed him from the team roster.

NO PROBLEM

Hall of Fame offensive lineman Gene Upshaw had a basic approach to football. "I have to laugh at these guys who make offense sound like a science," said Upshaw. "They sit at a blackboard all day drawing their diagrams like kids trying to pass algebra. Hey! There's no secret to offense. If you're a lineman, just fire out and knock the man in front of you down."

STRIP SHOW

The Philadelphia Eagles were coached by Dick Vermeil in the 1980s. Vermeil was a perfectionist who sometimes ran out of patience too quickly. In 1980, a free-agent guard reported to the Eagles' pre-season camp and quickly got on Vermeil's bad side. The Eagles' head coach lost his patience with the young guard and demanded that the new player be cut from the squad right in the middle of practice—which he was! When the free agent received the bad news, the young guard decided to exit in style by upstaging his former coach. The recently released player walked off the playing field, stripping off equipment bit by bit as he headed for the locker room. In the wake of his hasty retreat, he left behind pads, pants, a chin strap, and everything else. When the player finally reached the locker room, he was dressed only in his shorts!

SCHOOL'S OUT

Defensive lineman John Matuszak liked playing for the Oakland Raiders because there were few team rules to restrict his free-spirited ways. "Hey! You treat men like men and they play like men," said Matuszak after Oakland won Super Bowl XV in 1981. "If you treat them like boys, they play like boys."

WACKY RUNNERS AND RECEIVERS

AGE RACE

When Joe Sulaitis was a young rookie with the New York Giants, he played defense against fullback Bronko Nagurski of the Chicago Bears. Nagurski, who had a reputation as a ferocious player, looked across the line of scrimmage at Sulaitis.

"Now, take it easy on an old man," Bronko pleaded with Joe as he got into his stance. The ball was snapped and it was handed off to Nagurski. Bronko bolted through the line, smashed into Joe Sulaitis, and knocked him flat. Sulaitis lay in a stunned heap as old man Bronko Nagurski rumbled on down the field.

FENDER BENDER

Receiver Gerald Riggs of the Washington Redskins had quite a head-on collision in 1989. The six-foot, 232–pound Riggs went out for a pass in practice and smashed into a pickup truck parked near the sidelines. Gerald walked away from the accident unhurt, but the truck wasn't as lucky. Riggs inflicted $1,370 worth of damage to the pickup, including a severely dented door and a broken window.

SHOE THING

Emmitt Smith, the star running back for the Dallas Cowboys, had quite a game on October 31, 1993. Smith rushed for 237 yards on 30 carries in a 23–10 victory over the Philadelphia

Eagles. Emmitt's 237 yards was a Cowboys record and tied with Jim Brown for the sixth-best single-game rushing mark ever posted in the history of the National Football League. To celebrate his feat, Emmitt Smith retired the shoes he wore in the contest to his own personal Hall of Fame.

HOW SWEET

Walter Payton is one of the NFL's all-time great rushers. However, the former Chicago Bear wasn't known for his ferocity. In fact, Walter's nickname was "Sweetness." How did Payton get that curious nickname? One day in college, he was running up and down the field making great fakes and agile cuts. Players watching him perform said, "How sweet it is!" After that, teammates started calling Walter Payon "Sweetness," and the name stuck!

LOSING HIS HEAD

Getting to the Super Bowl is the goal of every NFL player. When the Buffalo Bills met the Washington Redskins in the 1992 Super Bowl contest (Super Bowl XXVI), star running back Thurman Thomas of the Bills sort of lost his head. Thurman missed playing the first two offensive plays of the day for Buffalo, for a strange reason. Thomas misplaced his helmet on the sidelines and didn't find it until the Bills had already run two plays. Washington, however, had no trouble finding its offense that day and topped Buffalo 37 to 24.

UNFAIR ODDS

Bill Hewitt, who played in the 1930s, was one of pro football's greatest stars at tight end. After he played for the Chicago Bears for several years, he was traded to the Philadelphia Eagles. When the Bears met the Eagles in regular-season play, Hewitt's old teammates tried to neutralize Bill right from the start. On the first play from scrimmage, they triple-teamed him and knocked him to the ground. But Bill Hewitt wasn't the kind of player who could be easily intimidated. He jumped right up and yelled at his former Bears teammates, "Three men on one end? Haven't you guys any confidence in yourselves?"

NO THANKS

Green Bay Packers flanker Caroll Dale described what it felt like to catch a pass in a big game. "My best moment is getting open and catching the ball, but it's no big thrill," said Dale. "I'm just thankful I didn't drop it."

LAST LAUGH

It was a long season for Pat Stoqua of the Canadian Football League's Ottawa Rough Riders in 1981. Pat, a wide receiver, didn't snare a single touchdown toss during the entire regular season. However, he made up for his lack of touchdown grabs in a play-off game against the Hamilton Tiger-Cats. He caught a 102-yard touchdown pass!

SETTING THE TABLE

In 1985, outstanding receiver Irving Fryar of the New England Patriots injured his thumb at home a week before the AFC Championship. Fryar's thumb was accidentally cut with a knife. The following year, Fryar was involved in a minor car accident on his way to practice because he took a wrong turn when the road he was on came to a fork. After the auto incident, a line in the sports section of a New–England–based newspaper described Irving Fryar's frequent mishaps this way: "First the knife in the kitchen—now the fork in the road."

YOU BET!

Jim Thorpe was a great star for one of pro football's earliest teams, the Canton Bulldogs. One of Canton's toughest rivals in those days was a team known as the Massillon Tigers. Jim Thorpe was sometimes known to bet on his own team to win. Back in the early 1900s, it was legal to wager on pro games, and players often added to their meager salaries by doing so.

In 1916, the Bulldogs and Tigers met in back-to-back games. In the first contest, Canton's biggest star, Jim Thorpe, was injured and the game ended in a scoreless tie. Football fans expected Canton to easily win the rematch, until they heard a rumor that Jim Thorpe was still hurt and would not play in the second game. Of course, the odds against Canton winning that contest went way up. However, Thorpe did play in the game. The Bulldogs walloped the Tigers 23–0, and Thorpe scored all of Canton's points. Later, it was learned that Thorpe had made a hefty wager on his team to win. It was also suspected, but never proven, that the person who spread the rumor that the great Jim Thorpe was hurt and could not play against Massillon in that second game was Jim Thorpe himself.

SMALL FRY

New York Jets wide receiver Wayne Chrebet snared 150 passes in his first two NFL seasons (1995 and 1996). What makes Chrebet's stats even more impressive is that Wayne is only five feet, ten inches tall and weighs only 180 pounds! In his first year as a Jet in 1995, he had some trouble getting into the Jets' training camp. A security guard at the gate did not believe he was a pro football player. The guard thought the undersized Wayne Chrebet was just an autograph seeker.

GOING, GOING, GONE!

In November 1973, receiver Johnny Rogers of the Montreal Alouettes caught a last-second touchdown pass that sealed a win against the Toronto Argonauts in a Canadian Football League contest. Rogers celebrated his spectacular grab by tossing the ball to appreciative fans in the stands. When the two teams lined up for the PAT (the point after try), the officials noticed a problem. There was no ball! Johnny Rogers had tossed the very last game ball into the stands. The contest had to be concluded without such an attempt being made.

NO BRAINER

Duane Thomas is one of the Dallas Cowboys' all-time great

running backs, but no one ever accused him of being a nuclear scientist. When someone questioned him about his I.Q., Thomas replied, "Sure I've got one. It's a perfect 20/20."

BAD BOUNCE!

In a Monday Night Football game between the Pittsburgh Steelers and the Kansas City Chiefs on October 18, 1972, receiver Dave Smith of the Steelers made the ultimate goof. Smith hauled in a pass which should have been an easy touchdown. As he sped toward the end zone, he spiked the ball in triumph. Unfortunately, Smith's gesture was premature. He accidentally spiked the ball before he crossed the goal line. The ball bounced on the five-yard line and rolled into the end zone for a touchback instead of a touchdown. The Chiefs took possession of the pigskin and went on to win the contest 38–16.

ROYAL TREATMENT

The 1983 Super Bowl (Super Bowl XVII) matched the Washington Redskins against the Miami Dolphins. The Redskins, led by running back John Riggins, beat the Dolphins 27–17 to win the NFL crown. Riggins, who gained a then Super Bowl record of 166 yards on 38 carries, was named the Most Valuable Player of the gridiron contest.

After the game, President Ronald Reagan called John Riggins on the phone to congratulate him on the victory and his personal accomplishments. After speaking with the commander-in-chief, Riggins hung up the phone and said, "Ronald Reagan may be president, but today I'm king."

HAT TRICK

Philadelphia Eagles wide receiver Mike Quick was a guy who

used his head to take up a hobby. Mike Quick's hobby was collecting all types of caps and hats.

SHOE THING

Pro football's Hall-of-Famer Johnny ("Blood") McNally was a star back for the Green Bay Packers, the Pittsburgh Steelers, and other pro football teams in the 1930s. When Johnny laced up his football spikes, he skipped every other hole because it brought him luck.

FILM STARS

During their flamboyant careers as a starting fullback and tailback for the Miami Dolphins, Larry Csonka and Jim Kiick were known by the nicknames Butch Cassidy and the Sundance Kid, because they were always on the run.

THE HILARIOUS HUDDLE

OLD STORY

The truth is, professional football is a game for young men. No one knew that better than New York Giants quarterback Charlie Conerly, who played in the 1950s. "When you win, you're an old pro," said Conerly to reporters. "When you lose, you're an old man!"

POLITICALLY INCORRECT

"Dandy" Don Meredith starred as quarterback for the Dallas Cowboys and later in the broadcast booth as pro football analyst. When Meredith worked as a sports announcer on ABC's Monday Night Football contests, he was often blunt. One evening, United States Vice President Spiro Agnew visited the broadcast booth during a game. Dandy Don greeted the Vice President by saying, "I didn't vote for you, but you do have a nice suit on."

HATS OFF!

When Fred Smerlas was a player for the Buffalo Bills, his favorite prank was to go into the locker room early and fill up his teammates' helmets with shaving cream.

SNAP DECISION

Renowned running back Gale Sayers quickly impressed many people during his rookie season with the Chicago Bears in 1965. Sayers had big games against most opposing defenders. However, when the Bears played the Green Bay Packers that year, Sayers found some old pros were unimpressed by his gridiron heroics. During the game, Gale took a pitchout and started around the Packers' line on a sweep play. Defensive end Willie Davis and middle linebacker Ray Nitschke converged on Sayers and sandwiched the Bears runner between them. Somehow, Gale Sayers ended up in the air with Davis holding one of his legs and Nitschke holding the other. "Okay, Ray," Gale Sayers heard Willie Davis say, "make a wish, baby!"

THAT STINKS!

In 1997, members of the Arizona Cardinals played a practical joke on teammate Jake Plummer. They removed a dead skunk from the side of the road and put it in Jake's room during training camp.

PUNCHY

George Trafton was a standout for the old Chicago Bears (1922–1932). Trafton, who was named All-NFL center 13 times, was a tough and crafty athlete who knew how to get the best of opposing players. One afternoon, the Bears and the Chicago Cardinals (who later moved to St. Louis) were battling it out on the gridiron. A big, young center on the Cardinals was beating up on George at every opportunity. Trafton warned the center to stop with the cheap shots, but the Cardinals player didn't heed his words.

To teach the young player a lesson, George Trafton waited until there was a big pileup. Then he punched the center right in the face. (In those days, there were no face masks on helmets.) Since the players were piled up, the referee didn't see the punch. After he socked the opposing player, George Trafton jumped up and ran over to the referee. "Watch that Cardinals center," he told the ref. "He keeps punching me." On the next play, the Cardinals' center was so angry with George Trafton that he threw a punch at him. Alerted by Trafton's warning, the referee was watching the play closely. He quickly paced off a 15-yard penalty against the Cardinals, and George Trafton got a double dose of revenge!

SIT-DOWN PAY

Just how good was fullback Bronko Nagurski of the Chicago Bears? In the early 1930s, Nagurski had such great games against the Detroit Lions that Lions owner Dick Richards had a meeting with Bronko and George Halas, the owner of the Bears. Richards offered Bronko Nagurski a check for $10,000. "I'm not trying to sign you," Richards said to Bronko as Halas looked on. "I just don't want you to play." Richards was willing to pay the Bears star $10,000 to sit out the 1935 season. George Halas was happy when Bronko Nagurski returned the check to Dick Richards. In the long run, the strange offer really didn't matter. The Detroit Lions won the NFL title in 1935.

MEAL TICKET

In 1995, head coach Dennis Erickson of the Seattle Seahawks fined Seattle players Rick Mirer, Cortez Kennedy, and Eugene Robinson $1,000 each for their behavior in a pre-season game against the San Francisco 49ers. What mistake did Mirer, Kennedy, and Robinson make? Erickson caught them eating hot dogs on the sidelines during the NFL contest!

HAIR TODAY, GONE TOMORROW

Rookies who arrive at pre-season football camps often have pranks played on them by NFL veterans. In 1997, members of the Tennessee Oilers went a bit too far when the Oiler veterans tried to cut up rookie defensive end Brent Burnstein's long hair. Burnstein refused to be the recipient of this prank, so he packed up his gear and left training camp. He was later picked up by the Arizona Cardinals, who promised Brent that the Cardinals veterans would leave his long locks alone. The Cardinals eventually cut him.

FAST TALKER

Vince Lombardi's Green Bay Packers suffered through a dismal scoring slump in 1965. The usually offensive-minded Packers scored a measly 36 points over a span of four games. An angry Vince Lombardi quickly called a team meeting after the fourth low-scoring contest.

"Gentlemen, we're going back to basics," grumbled Lombardi to his squad. "We're going to work on fundamentals." Vince help up a pigskin. "This is a football," he shouted to the startled Packers.

Jokester Max McGee, a Green Bay receiver, raised his hand and stood up. "Slow down, coach," Max teased, "you're going too fast."

SEE YA'

Quarterback Troy Aikman was named to the 1993 Pro Bowl, which took place at Aloha Stadium, in Hawaii. Although the Dallas quarterback was pleased by the honor, he packed up his gear and left early in the fourth quarter of the game. Troy claimed that he exited the contest before it was over because he had to catch an early flight out of Hawaii in order to make a scheduled meeting in Dallas the next day. Aikman later apologized to NFL fans for his hasty exit from the Pro Bowl.

TALL ORDER

In 1981, five-foot, ten-inch cornerback Terry Jackson of the New York Giants was expected to cover six-foot, eight-inch receiver Harold Carmichael of the Philadelphia Eagles in an upcoming game. Before the gridiron clash began, reporters asked Jackson how he felt about his tough assignment. "I went out to lunch the other day," said Terry Jackson, "and about twenty people offered to lend me their stepladders."

WHO'S LEAVING?

The Dallas Cowboys' defense came up with an ingenious way to confuse the potent Washington Redskins' offense during a game in 1985. The Cowboys kept an extra defensive player in the game until just before the snap of the ball. The 12th defender would then sprint off so the Cowboys would not be penalized. The last-minute dash confused the Washington offense because they never knew which players were staying in the game until it was too late to alter the offensive call.

YOU BET

Alex Karras was one of the NFL's all-time great defensive players. Karras was once suspended from playing in the NFL for making small wagers on his Detroit Lions team. After he returned to play for the Lions, Karras was named team captain. Alex was on the field for the coin toss when the referee prepared to flip the coin. "You call it, Captain Karras," the ref said to Alex.

"Sorry, ref, but I can't," Alex answered without cracking a smile. "You know I'm not allowed to gamble."

SMELL THE ROSES

Fullback Jim Brown of the Cleveland Browns and linebacker Sam Huff of the New York Giants had some intense personal match-ups during their long NFL careers. One day, the Browns were deep in Giants territory when Jim Brown got the handoff. Sam Huff sliced through the Cleveland offensive line and dropped Jim for a two-yard loss.

"Ha!" scoffed Huff as he got up. "You stink, Jim."

On the next play, Jim Brown got the ball again. This time, he smashed through the Giants' defense to score a Cleveland touchdown. "Hey, Sam!" Brown yelled to Huff. "How do I smell from here?"

NO CONFIDENCE

Atlanta Falcons head coach Dan Henning put his foot in his mouth in 1986 while talking to reporters about young starting quarterback David Archer's performance on the field. Henning didn't exactly boost Archer's confidence when he said, "They ought to send David to Washington. He can over-throw any government."

EXTRA HELP

Pro football games are watched intensely by officials, coaches, players, and fans. So why didn't anyone notice something was amiss when the Detroit Lions beat the Dallas Cowboys on a last-second field goal in November 1981? Detroit kicker Eddie Murray's 47-yard field goal at the gun nipped Dallas by the score of 27–24. It wasn't until Cowboy coaches reviewed the game's films after the contest that anyone noticed that the Lions had 12 men on the field during the play instead of the regulation 11 players. Strangely enough, the side judge who goofed by not counting the Lions players in the field was a former Dallas running back who played for the Cowboys in the 1960s.

REMEMBER THIS!

Quarterback Bobby Layne, who won championships with the Detroit Lions in 1952, 1953, and 1957, had no sympathy for offensive players who blew assignments. "I don't care if a guy tries to make a block and gets beat," Layne once said. "But I can't stand a guy who forgets an assignment. They get paid good money to remember!"

PAY UP

In 1994, the San Francisco 49ers signed cornerback and superstar athlete Deion Sanders to a one-year, 1.134-million-dollar contract which included a $750,000 bonus if the 49ers competed in the Super Bowl. In order to sign Sanders, All-Pro wide receiver Jerry Rice of San Francisco had to give up $170,000 in incentive bonus money. When asked about his monetary loss, Rice replied, "Are you kidding? Just

$170,000 not to have Deion guarding me twice a year? That's cheap!"

DEFENSIVE COMMENT

Allie Sherman was the head coach of the New York Giants during the 1960s. Sherman had some good and some bad years with the Giants. During one of the bad years, Sherman was rushing out of a hotel in New York when he bumped into an old sports fan, knocking off the guy's hat. "Sorry, sir," apologized Sherman as he fetched the man's hat. "No offense."

The man, who quickly recognized Allie Sherman as the Giants' coach, nodded. "You're telling me," the man replied. "That's been your trouble all season."

SKY HIGH

The Baltimore Colts had a secret weapon for their game against the Washington Redskins during the 1960 NFL season. That weapon was wide receiver R.C. Owens, who had been a basketball player and was still a great leaper. Owens and his coach, Weeb Ewbank, had tried out a bizarre way to block field goals in practice, and the wacky scheme seemed to work. R.C. stood back beneath the goalpost, and if the field-goal kicker's boot was close enough to the crossbar he jumped up and deflected the pigskin before it could sail through the uprights.

The nutty plan actually worked in an NFL contest. When Washington kicker Bob Khayat attempted a 40-yard field goal against the Colts in 1960, R.C. Owens was ready. Positioned beneath the crossbar, he jumped up and knocked the field-goal attempt off course. Unfortunately, however, this wacky way of blocking field goals only worked that one time.

BUS-TRIPPED

When Dick Vermeil was coaching the Philadelphia Eagles, he was a strict disciplinarian. Players usually didn't care to test his authority. One Saturday, Eagles players Bill Bergey, Frank LeMaster, and John Bunting went out to eat before catching the team bus for a game against the Giants in New Jersey on Sunday. Bergey ordered a special pizza that took so long to prepare that the three defensive stars missed the team bus. Bergey, Bunting, and LeMaster all knew that missing the bus was an automatic $500 fine. They were also worried about facing the wrath of coach Vermeil. Quickly, Bergey came up with a plan. The Eagles hopped into Bill Bergey's car and raced from Philadelphia to the New Jersey hotel where the Eagles would be staying. The team was already there when the three latecomers drove into the hotel's basement parking lot. Bill Bergey, John Bunting, and Frank LeMaster took the elevator from the parking lot to the lobby, where the other Philadelphia players and coaches were standing around. Bergey, Bunting, and LeMaster quietly blended into the crowd. Coach Vermeil, the strict disciplinarian, had never missed them, and they each saved five hundred dollars in fines.

WORN OUT

The great Charlie Conerly played 13 years at quarterback for the New York Giants and guided his squad to numerous victories. After the 1961 NFL season, Charlie decided it was time for him to retire from pro football. Conerly described what it was like to be an aging pro in the NFL to a reporter. "It takes longer to recover after playing on Sunday," Charlie explained. "I used to feel pretty good again by Tuesday. Then it was Wednesday, and later, Thursday. Now, it's Saturday before I get over it. That's the years."

PLANE CRAZY

In 1985, the Chicago Bears' defensive lineman, William the "Fridge" Perry, who weighed almost 350 pounds, was scheduled to appear as a guest on the "David Letterman Show." When New York Jets personnel director Mike Hickey heard the "Fridge" was flying into New York City, he asked, "When they fly Perry in, is he in the cargo bin?"

WAKE-UP CALL

Joe Stydahar, the head coach of the Los Angeles Rams, was a big, likeable man who had a hot temper. In the 1951 NFL pre-season, the Rams played the Philadelphia Eagles at Little Rock, Arkansas. Surprisingly, Los Angeles topped Philadelphia to score a big upset win. The Rams players were so happy they went out after the game to celebrate. Stydahar didn't mind the celebration until it turned into an all-night

shindig. When Joe checked the players' rooms at 2:00 a.m., most of his veterans were missing. He started phoning local nightclubs in an attempt to locate his athletes. In order to fool the Rams players into answering his calls, he pretended to be a Los Angeles player. He knew no Rams athlete would want to talk to his irate head coach.

After many calls, Coach Stydahar located veteran guard Jack Finlay at a club. Still pretending to be a player, Stydahar asked Finlay, "Is anyone else with you?"

"Sure," Finlay replied. "We're all here. Come on over."

"Listen, Finlay," the coach yelled into the phone. "This is Stydahar. You guys have 30 minutes to get back to the hotel. You're all fined $100 each and if it takes you longer than 30 minutes to get here, I'll fine you all another $100 each!" He then hung up.

BACKWARDS, TOO?

In 1985, kicker Rafael Septien of the Dallas Cowboys missed a short field goal. When the coach asked Septien how he could miss such an easy kick, Rafael placed the blame on holder Danny White. "I missed it because the ball was placed upside down," Rafael Septien explained.

HAT TRICK

Curly Lambeau, the coach of the Green Bay Packers (1919–1949), insisted that it was bad luck for him to wear the same hat to more than one NFL game. Lambeau always wore a different hat to each and every NFL contest. Curly also had another habit which contributed to his hat superstition. Whenever things went wrong for the Packers during a game, he would twist and pull his hat apart with his hands.

HOT DOG!

The Philadelphia Eagles faced the Oakland Raiders in Super Bowl XV in 1981. The game was played in New Orleans, which proved to be a homecoming for Eagles wide receiver Rodney Parker. Parker, a native of New Orleans, had been present at the first Super Bowl game ever played in New Orleans. However, Parker didn't get to enjoy much of the Kansas City Chiefs' 23–7 win over the Minnesota Vikings in Super Bowl IV in 1969. Teenage Rodney Parker was busy in the stands working as a hotdog vendor. Unfortunately for Rodney, he didn't enjoy his trip home in 1981. Oakland beat Philadelphia 27–10 in Super Bowl XV.

CRAZY COACHES

QUICK SCORE

When the Washington Redskins were known as the Boston Redskins in the 1930s, the head coach of the squad was a zany, full-blooded Native American named Lone Star Dietz. One afternoon, the Redskins were playing the New York Giants at Fenway Park in Boston. Before Dietz started up a ramp that led from the field to the stadium press box, he met with his team captains. "If we win the coin toss," Coach Dietz said, "elect to kick off to the Giants."

The captains nodded and Lone Star Dietz started up to the press box. He was unable to see the field during his ascent, but he did hear the stadium announcer say that the Redskins had won the toss. After a long climb through the bowels of the stadium, he reached the press box. When he got his next view of the field, Dietz was astonished to see his team lining up to receive the kickoff. "What the heck!" he yelled. "I told those guys to kick off if we won the toss."

One of the Washington assistant coaches walked up to Lone Star Dietz and said, "We did, coach. Where have you been? The Giants are already ahead seven to nothing."

JUST PARK IT HERE

When Tom Landry was coaching the Dallas Cowboys, some players regarded him as a gridiron demi-god. Cowboys linebacker Steve Kiner was not as impressed. When Kiner was a rookie, Landry drove to practice and found Kiner's car parked in the special place reserved for the car belonging to the Cowboys' head coach. After Coach Landry tracked down the young linebacker in the locker room, Landry's first words to him were, "I admire a man with courage."

WORRIED LOOK?

Green Bay Packers head coach Vince Lombardi once said, "A real executive goes around with a worried look on his assistants."

YUK!

In 1990, the Indianapolis Colts began the season with three straight losses. "When you see that big zero up there for wins," said Colts coach Ron Meyer, "it's like somebody put a dead rat in your mouth."

TOUGH BREAK

Dan Devine's head coaching debut in the NFL in 1970 was spoiled by the New York Giants in more ways than one. In Devine's first game as an NFL head coach, the Giants edged Devine's Green Bay Packers squad by the score of 42 to 40. To add injury to insult, coach Devine was injured in the game. During the gridiron clash, a Giants player ran out of bounds and smashed into the Packers' head coach, breaking Devine's leg. The Green Bay coach had to be carried away from his first NFL coaching contest on a stretcher.

DON'T BE A LOSER

Coach George Halas of the Chicago Bears may not have believed that winning was everything, but he had an interesting motto. George Halas' motto was: "Always go to bed a winner!"

BORN-AGAIN FOOTBALL

George Allen, the former coach of the Washington Redskins who led them to their first Super Bowl appearance in 1972, believed a football game was something mystical. "Every time you win, you're reborn," preached Allen, "and when you lose you die a little."

MINUTE MAN

There are many funny stories about how tough Green Bay Packers coach Vince Lombardi was on his players in training camp. Once, Lombardi made a rule that all of his players had to be in bed by eleven o'clock during training. One evening, star defensive back Emlen Tunnell—who was later elected to the Hall of Fame—walked into the team dorm at one minute to eleven. Tunnell was shocked to find Coach Lombardi waiting for him. "You're late. That'll be a $50 fine," Vince told Emlen.

"But Coach," argued Tunnell, "it's not eleven o'clock yet."

Lombardi looked Tunnell right in the eyes. Without batting an eyelash, Vince said, "Em, you know you can't be in bed with your clothes off in one minute." Emlen Tunnell just shook his head and agreed to pay the money.

NO BONUS CLAUS

When Vince Lombardi was coach of the Green Bay Packers, he ate, drank, and slept football twenty-four hours a day. Once, during the holiday season, an assistant coach asked if he could leave a coaches' meeting a bit early to do some Christmas shopping. Lombardi quickly denied the request. "Do you want to be Santa Claus or a football coach?" Vince snapped. "There's no room for both."

FINE WITH ME

Green Bay Packers head coach Vince Lombardi was often forced to fine his free-spirited tight end Max McGee for various rule infractions. On one occasion, Vince fined Max $250 for breaking a team rule. A short time later, Lombardi cited McGee for another rule infraction, and the second fine was upped to $500. After he levied the $500 fine, Lombardi cautioned his tight end to pay more attention to rules. "The next fine will be $1000, Max," said Vince. "But if you find anything worth a thousand-buck fine, let me know and I'll go with you."

THANKS, COACH

Lone Star Dietz, the Native-American head coach of the old Boston Redskins, liked to upstage other pro football coaches. One year, the Chicago Bears traveled to Boston to play the

Redskins. The Bears' innovative head coach, George Halas, scheduled a big meeting before the game. The meeting was held in a conference room at the hotel where the Bears were staying, and was restricted to Chicago personnel.

In a dimly lit room, Coach Halas stood in a spotlight and pointed out to his squad what the Bears had to do to beat Boston. The Bears' coach told his players where and how the Redskins' defense was vulnerable to the Bears' offense. He also went over what the Chicago defense had to do to prevent the Redskins' offense from scoring. At the end of the meeting, the lights in the room were turned on. A man in the front row stood up. "Thanks, Coach," said the man as he stretched. "All of that was very helpful." The man was Lone Star Dietz, the coach of the Boston Redskins. Somehow, Dietz had managed to sneak into the private meeting,

BUG OFF!

The New York Giants played the Chicago Bears in the 1941 NFL Championship game. During the contest, Ben Sohn, a Giants lineman, had his football jersey grabbed by a Bears player and ripped off. Steve Owen, the New York coach, raced up to the referee.

"Are you blind?" he yelled. "The Bears were holding Sohn."

The referee refused to argue with the Giants' head coach. Calmly, the ref turned his back to Owen and walked away. "Maybe I was wrong," Steve Owen called after the escaping referee. "Maybe the Bears didn't rip Sohn's jersey off. Maybe it was moths!" By the way, Chicago beat New York 31–9.

NOT PICTURE-PERFECT

In early December 1993, Miami Dolphins coach Don Shula was named *Sports Illustrated*'s Man of the Year. His picture appeared on the magazine's cover. Shula seemed like a good choice at the time. His team's record at Thanksgiving was 9–2, and Miami appeared to be headed for the playoffs. All the Dolphins had to do to make the playoffs was to win one of their last five games. Unfortunately, the Dolphins lost all five games. After his picture appeared on the cover of *Sports Illustrated*, Don Shula did not win another NFL game that season, and his team didn't make it to the playoffs.

NO EGO

Head coach Jim Lee Howell of the New York Giants never had any ego problems, even though he guided the Giants to the 1956 NFL Championship. On Howell's staff during his reign as head coach were two future great NFL coaches: Tom Landry and Vince Lombardi. Once a reporter asked Jim Lee how he organized his time as the Giants' head coach. "I really don't do anything," Howell replied. "If I want to know something about defense, I ask Landry. If I want to know something about offense, I ask Lombardi. My job on this team is to make sure the players are in bed by curfew and to blow up all the footballs we need on Sunday."

SAND-TRAP PLAY

Dick Vermeil was an NFL coach who never stopped thinking about football. To take breaks from the rigors of coaching, Dick occasionally played golf. In 1980, while Vermeil was head coach of the Philadelphia Eagles, he was playing golf with a friend. Dick whacked one of his shots into a sand trap. Instead of blasting his ball out of the sand trap, Coach Vermeil knelt down and began to scratch X's and O's in the sand with a club. A few minutes later he had completely sketched out a football play that had just popped into his head.

ARE YOU KIDDING, COACH?

When the San Francisco 49ers arrived at their hotel prior to the 1982 Super Bowl, the players had to deal with an obnoxious bellboy who kept trying to wrestle their suitcases away from them. Several San Francisco players almost lost their temper with him. It was a good thing they didn't. After a closer look, players recognized the wiseguy bellboy. It was none other than San Francisco head coach Bill Walsh, playing a practical joke on his squad. By the way, the 49ers went on to beat the Cincinnati Bengals 26–21.

THANKS A LOT, POP!

On October 2, 1994, the first father–son coaching match-up in the history of the NFL took place. Head coach Don Shula's Miami Dolphins took on the Cincinnati Bengals, coached by young Dave Shula, Don Shula's son. In the game, dear old dad had no mercy on his boy as the Dolphins trashed the Bengals 23–7.

NO RESPECT

In 1992, Bill Cowher was named head coach of the Pittsburgh Steelers. At an NFL coaches meeting in March 1992, Bill didn't get much respect. His name was spelled wrong on a place card at the breakfast table. Coach Cowhers' name was misspelled "Cower."

GUTSY CALL

An appendectomy operation didn't keep San Francisco 49ers defensive coach Ray Rhodes out of action in 1990. Rhodes coached the 49ers' defensive secondary from his hospital room using a television and a special telephone hookup. He was able to communicate with injured cornerback Eric

Wright and safety Chet Brooks on the San Francisco sidelines. Wright and Brooks then relayed Rhodes' signals to the players out on the field. This wacky coaching system worked as the 49ers' defensive secondary allowed just 14 Giant completions in San Francisco's 7–3 win.

BYE, GUYS

In his rush to get to a Super Bowl game, Oakland Raiders head coach John Madden had the team bus leave so early that several key members of his team were left back at the hotel. Luckily, the players who were left behind were able to hitch a ride to the stadium and arrived in time for the Super Bowl contest.

THANK GOD

Chuck Noll won four Super Bowls while he was the head coach of the Pittsburgh Steelers (IX, X, XIII, and XIV), but his career in Pittsburgh wasn't always rosy. In 1969, under Coach Noll, the Steelers won their first game and then lost 13 in a row. Things were so bad that season that a Pittsburgh player claimed Chuck Noll called Dial-A-Prayer for guidance and when he identified himself as the head coach of the Pittsburgh Pirates the line went dead.

WATCH OUT

Coach Sam Rutigliano of the Cleveland Browns once described Oakland Raiders owner Al Davis. "Al Davis is the king of guy who would steal your eyes," said Rutigliano, "and then try to convince you that you looked better without them."

NICE GUY?

When Mike Ditka, the outspoken NFL coach, was hired by the New Orleans Saints in 1997, he tried to explain his usual candor to the press. "Hey! When you're winning and you say something, it's cute," said Ditka. "But when you're losing and you say something, you're an idiot."

SORRY, DAD

During the 1985 season, Wade Phillips succeeded his father "Bum" Phillips as the head coach of the New Orleans Saints. Bum Phillips was so unpopular with the New Orleans fans that Wade Phillips thought he needed some help if he were to remain as coach of the Saints. So Wade jokingly started a rumor that he was adopted.

A FOOT IN THE MOUTH

In the mid-1960s, pro football teams became obsessed with long-range soccer-style kickers. Soccer-style booters of all shapes and sizes were given pro football tryouts to prove their ability to split the uprights as potential NFL field-goal kickers. An Englishman visiting the United States was granted a tryout by the New York Jets' head coach, Weeb Ewbank, sight unseen. The Englishman showed up at the stadium for his NFL trial with his agent.

When Coach Ewbank came out on the field, he found a tall, young blond fellow standing next to a short, pudgy bald guy in his late 40s. "Let's see what this soccer player of yours can do," Weeb said to the bald guy. "If he's good, we'll discuss a contract."

"Just a second, Coach," interrupted the young fellow. "I'm the agent. He's the kicker."

POOR GUY

Former Houston Oilers coach Bum Phillips may not have been fast on his feet, but he was always quick-witted. "Our land was so poor when I was a kid," Bum once said, "we had to fertilize the house just to raise the windows."

BOTTOMS UP!

When Ray Malavasi entered his second year as head coach of the Los Angeles Rams, he told reporters that his approach to the game was basically the same as before. "I said when I became head coach that I wouldn't change," Ray stated. I don't think I have. I still drink at the same bars."

COLD WORDS

Former NFL Dallas Cowboys coach Tom Landry was considered by many football fans to be stoic and completely without emotion. Someone once joked, "If the *Titanic* hit Tom Landy, it would sink."

INDEX

Huff, Sam, 54, 73

I

Indianapolis Colts, 18, 46, 81
"I shall return," 18

J

Jackson, Terry, 72
Jeter, Gary, 27
Johnson, Johnny, 28
Jones, David "Deacon," 48, 49, 54
Jordan, Lee Roy, 52

K

Kansas City Chiefs, 12, 21, 25, 65
Karras, Alex, 32, 73
Kasay, John, 46
Kennedy, Cortez, 70
Kenney, Bill, 12, 13
Khayat, Bob, 75
Kiick, Jim, 66
Kincaid, Pete and Bonnie, 44
Kiner, Steve, 80, 81

L

Lambeau, Curly, 79
Lambert, Jack, 40
Landeta, Sean, 34
Landry, Tom, 80, 81, 85, 89
Laufenberg, Babe, 15
Layne, Bobby, 8, 74
League of Women Voters, 38
LeBaron, Eddie, 11, 12
LeMaster, Frank, 76, 77
Leonard, Jim, 29
Letterman, David, 24, 77
Lewin, Dennis, 41, 42
Lewis, Leo, 27
Lilly, Bob, 55, 56
Linemen, 55-59
  Donovan, Art, 56, 58
  Golic, Bob, 55
  Greene, Kevin, 56
  Holmes, Lester, 57
  Lilly, Bob, 55, 56

  Mansfield, Ray, 56
  Matuszak, John, 55, 59
  Newton, Nate, 56
  Olsen, Bob, 57
  Upshaw, Gene, 58, 59
  Washington, Russ, 57
Lipscomb, Eugene "Big Daddy," 48
Lipski, John "Bull," 35
Lombardi, Vince, 21, 36, 40, 70, 81, 82, 83, 85
Los Angeles Raiders, 13
Los Angeles Rams, 11, 21, 28, 34, 44, 48, 51, 52, 57, 77, 78, 79, 89
Lucas, Harold, 38, 39

M

MacArthur, Douglas, 18
Madden, John, 87
Malavasi, Ray, 21, 89
Mann, Errol, 41
Mansfield, Ray, 56
Marchetti, Gino, 49
Marshall, Jim, 32, 50
Massillon Tigers, 63, 64
Masterson, Bernie, 17
Matuszak, John, 55, 59
McGee, Max, 71, 83
McInally, Pat, 22
McMahon, Jim, 17, 18
McNally, Johnny "Blood," 66
Meredith, Don, 42, 67
Meyer, Ron, 81
Miami Dolphins, 22, 31, 65, 66, 84, 85, 86
Michaels, Walt, 28
Michigan State, 38
Minnesota Vikings, 27, 29, 30, 32, 34, 50
Mirer, Rick, 70
Mitchell, Bobby, 49
Modell, Art, 39
Montreal Alouettes, 34, 64
Morton, Craig, 15
Municipal Stadium, 39

ABOUT THE AUTHOR

Michael J. Pellowski was a New Jersey high-school football All Star who accepted a full athletic scholarship to Rutgers University. At Rutgers, he started 29 consecutive varsity football games, including the gridiron contest that celebrated college football's 100th anniversary.

As a defensive end, Pellowski recorded 17 career sacks, and once had four sacks in a single game. In 1970, he captained the Rutgers defense and earned A.P. and E.C.A.C. All East Division One honors.

After professional football trials with the Montreal Alouettes and the New England Patriots, Pellowski played several years of semi-pro football for the Hartford Knights and the New Jersey Oaks. He has had over 30 sports books published.